SOMETIMES YOUR PRESENCE IS ENOUGH

A Personal Account of Participation
in Un Colloque sur le Thème
"Femmes et Religions"
Brussels, Belgium
March 11, 2001

Organized by M. Hervé Hasquin
Ministre-Président of the Government
of the French Community
of Wallonia-Brussels

BY SUSAN STUBBS HYATT

GOD'S WORD TO WOMEN, INC. * 2019
Grapevine, Texas 76051

*Publish, and set up a standard;
publish and conceal not (Jeremiah 50:2).*

SOMETIMES YOUR PRESENCE IS ENOUGH: A Personal Account of Participation in Un Colloque sur le Thème "Femmes et Religions," Brussels, Belgium, March 11, 2001 by Susan Stubbs Hyatt

An International Christian Women's Hall Publication

Published by God's Word to Women, Incorporated and Hyatt International Ministries, Incorporated

Mailing Address (2019)
P. O. Box 3877
Grapevine, TX 76099

Internet Addresses
Email: DrSueHyatt@live.com
Web Site: godswordtowomen.org
FaceBook:
facebook.com/groups/IntChristianWomensHallofFame/
facebook.com/groups/godswordtowomen/

Photographs are from the site of the event.
Front Cover: The Lobby of Le Plaza Hotel, Brussels
Back Cover: The Theatre in Le Plaza Hotel, Brussels

Cover and Book Design by Susan Stubbs Hyatt

ISBN 978-1-888435-39-9

✣ Contents ✣

1

An Opportunity

On February 21, 2001, I received an unexpected invitation from the President of the French Community of Belgium. I was invited to be a scholarly voice for North American Pentecostal and Charismatic Women at a one-day colloquium in Brussels, Belgium, on Women and Religions.

Since I had no desire to travel and since I was fully occupied with ministry at home in Texas, my first inclination was to decline. But as I sought the Lord, it became clear that this was not a luxurious privilege being afforded me. It was, rather, a responsibility that He would have me assume. So, I agreed to go.

I still held a secret hope that I would not be able to go because I did not have a valid passport. But when the Canadian Consulate in Dallas was willing to expedite the process in record time, I was left without excuse!

Obviously, the Lord had opened a wide, effectual door for me in Europe and I would go as the single voice of Pentecostal-Charismatic Christianity, not only in North America, but also in the world.

On Friday morning, March 9, I flew from Dallas-Fort Worth Int'l Airport, just a stone's throw from home. After 11 hours in the air, I arrived in Brussels on Saturday morning in time to adjust to the 7-hour time difference and attend the reception that evening.

The Site of the Colloquium
Le Plaza Hotel, Brussels, Belgium

2

The Site of the Event

As a guest of the Belgium government, I was treated like an ambassador. The host provided splendid accommodations for us participants from around the world in Le Plaza Hotel, also the site of the colloquium.

Built in 1930, this prestigious palace served as the German command center for Northern France and Belgium during the Nazi occupation. After the liberation, it served as the European command post for Sir Winston Churchill and the British High Command. Following the war, it became the hotel-of-choice of celebrities such as Maurice Chevalier and Brigitte Bardot.

Renovated in 1976, this exquisite 5-star hotel provided luxurious surroundings for the event. Its classic banquet room was the site of the Saturday evening reception. Several breakout rooms, equipped with translation booths for English, Dutch, and German, accommodated our round-table discussions on Sunday morning. That afternoon, the 900-seat theater-television studio was filled to capacity for the 5-hour televised debate.

The colloquium was the idea of M. Hervé Hasquin, Ministre-Président of the Government of the French

Community of Wallonia-Brussels, Belgium. Motivation for this intercultural dialogue came, in part, in response to the United Nations' designation of 2001 as *The Year of Dialogue Among Civilizations.* A representative of the Secretary-General at the United Nations Information Center in Brussels carried greetings to the assembly.

The precise date of the colloquium, March 11th, was chosen to coincide as closely as possible with the United Nation's *Day of the Woman* (March 8th).

The site of the event was strategic. Brussels is the headquarters of NATO, the capital of Belgium, and the capital of the European Union. It has been said, perhaps accurately, that in this age of globalization, what happens in Brussels ultimately affects the entire world.

In calling this "grand international colloquium," M. Hasquin provided an important platform for Europe and the world to hear about the status and concerns of women from women of the world's major religious groups.

The Site of the TV Debate
The Theatre at Le Plaza Hotel

The Lobby of Le Plaza Hotel

3

The Participants

Forty women from 20 nations participated in the colloquium. Of these, 9 represented Christianity; 15, Islam; and 8, Judaism. Three were agnostics; 1, a Hindu; and 2, Buddhists. Two were simply listed as "other."

Christian Women. The 9 Christian women came from 6 different nations, including France, Belgium, Rwanda, Peru, Chili, and the United States (yours truly). Several were theology or history professors. One was a social anthropologist in South America. Chantal, an executive member of the African Alliance of the YMCA from Rwanda, explained that many in her nation had left Christianity as a result of the horrendous war (1994). Indeed, how could "Christians" justify such racial and tribal hatred?

The most alive and friendly of the Christian women was Sister Noëlle Hausman, Mother Superior of the Sisters of the Sacred Heart of Mary in Belgium. She had entered the convent at 15 years of age by special permission of Léon Joseph Cardinal Seunens, the outstanding Belgian leader of the Roman Catholic Charismatic Renewal. I asked Noëlle if this meant that she was Charismatic, to which she replied, "Oh, no! I am afraid!" This, of course, opened the door for me to assure her of God's love for her!

MUSLIM WOMEN. Islamic presence was very much in the majority, with 15 Moslem women representing 10 different nations, including: Senegal, Djibouti, Niger, Tunisia, Morocco, Spain, France, Belgium, Serbia-Bosnia-Herzegovina, and Turkey. Several of these women were university professors and 3 were high-profile members of government, including the Minister of Culture in Senegal; the Minister for the Promotion of Women in the Republic of Djibouti, and Princess Maria-Theresa of Bourbon Parme in Spain. Another, Guldenay Sonumeut, was Director of Production and International News for the 24-hour TV News Network of Turkey. And Mariama Hima was the Ambassador to France for the Republic of Niger.

Generally speaking, the Muslim women tended to be strong, intelligent, and aggressive. Certainly, they were very different from the veiled Islamic women we see in American supermarkets! But I noticed that whenever I would pass by Hawa from Djibouti, she would draw her headcovering more securely over her head and face.

JEWISH WOMEN. The 8 Jewish women were typically confident and conversant. Some were history of religions professors. Others were leaders of national Jewish women's organizations and directors of Jewish cultural centers. One high profile theologian from Germany, Ruth Lapide, once travelled America with her theologian husband, teaching the Jewish background of the Gospels. At the time of the colloquium, she was working on ethical issues with the German government and had a German television program promoting the Bible.

OTHER WOMEN. Of the other women, 3 were agnostics. Ann Morelli was a professor of History of Religion at the Free University of Brussels. Annie De Wiest, a secular feminist, was the French Community's Director of the Office of Equal Opportunities. And Antoinette Spaak served as Belgium's Minister of State.

The lone Hindu representative was Madhu Kishwar, the Director of the Center for the Study of Social Development at J. Nehru University in New Delhi.

Anne De Goes and Mia Castelijn were Buddhist nuns, while two, Nair Saitry and Gulya Mizroeva, did not state religious preference. Nair was a dancer and choreographer while Gulya was a Tajikistan-born film-maker living in France.

4

The Program

Overview. The program was conducted in French with translation into English, Dutch, and German. Although I am quite proficient in reading and writing French, my speaking and audio comprehension skills leave much to be desired! Even with the voice of good translators coming through my headset, I feel I missed much of what was being said.

On Sunday morning, we were divided into four round-table discussion groups facilitated by TV news anchors and professional journalists. One group discussed the history of women in the various religions. Another group discussed the place and status of women in the different religions. A third group discussed the ways that religious women express themselves in their various cultures. Of the 10 participants in this group, none were Christians.

The fourth group—the one to which I was assigned—dealt with the question: Where are we and where are we going? Since the emphasis in the group tended to be political in the minds of the leaders, the ambassador and cabinet ministers were part of this group.

After a brief lunch break, we convened to the theater for the live, televised debate. I was impressed with the ornate theater and I was surprised by the enthusiastic crowd of 900 men and women who had gathered for the event. I detected among these Europeans a greater concern and more genuine caring for women than I had, to date, observed in North America.

Five Antinomies. As the debate opened, we were challenged to consider certain "underpinning principles" in the relationship between women and religion. These 5 basics, opposing elements that exist together within each religion and that are common to all world religions, include the following presuppositions:

All religions contain myths that posit the liberation of women against patriarchal militancy.

All religions claim texts that propose gender equality and texts that are gender-restrictive.

All religions display power struggles between male superiority, on the one hand, and so-called "mystical movements" ascribing equality, on the other.

Fundamentalism in all religions legalistically dictates that men must dominate while feminism calls for the creation of what is new, stating that the patriarchal text of fundamentalism is not appropriate.

Religion is seen as an obstacle to women's liberation, yet religion often is the place where women find liberty.

5

The Voices of Women

Overview. Although I am aware of the injustices and inequities that women around the world are suffering, simply because they are women, what the various women shared served to remind and further inform me. Here is some of what I heard.

In Djibouti, most women are still illiterate. Women do not have equal educational opportunities, and poverty continues to stifle any hope of progress toward a better life. Furthermore, although genital mutilation has been outlawed, the practice continues.

In Algeria, access to education and increased civic power are seen as the only means by which women can combat the persecution and suffering that they are experiencing under the Islamic fundamentalist regime. The Algerians have a saying: "Paradise is under the feet of women," to which a well-educated Algerian refugee woman responded, "Then lift your foot, please!"

In Niger, more than 9 out of 10 women cannot read. The Islamic fundamentalism of Iran, Iraq, and Saudi Arabia, through the power of oil money, is gaining increased control in these nations. Many women simply accept this, refusing to take responsibility for their personal development and settling instead for submission according to the family code of Islam. This whole situation is contributing to the suffering of women in many ways. Girls are no longer permitted education. Women are required to "adore their husbands" and are no longer allowed to be "fashionable," but must wear veils and long dresses. The Ambassador noted that women must take personal responsibility to improve their condition. In her opinion, the future of Africa is in the hands of women. Unfortunately, many who have the education to run for government positions no longer have the economic means to do so.

Melika Bosnawi, Islamic representative from Bosnia-Herzegovina, erupted with intense anger during the TV debate regarding the horrendous war crimes against Moslem women in her land. These atrocities, of which most of us are aware, reflect badly on Christendom.

The Minister of Culture of Senegal stated, "Mohammed came and brought liberty to women!" The problem, she explained, is that few women in her nation can read and therefore, in her opinion, cannot interpret the Islamic texts in terms that would bring the equality that Mohammed intended.

Princess Maria Theresa, a Moslem and highly educated social scientist, said, "Equality of women represents the future."

Hinduism, explained Madhu Kishwar, teaches a principle of feminine energy, a positive creative force which produces wealth. This leads to the possibility of two different kinds of women. One is a benevolent consort who is attached to a male and the other is a strong woman who is unattached to a male. She is understood to be seeking her own interests and men are expected to bow to her. Within the family structure, mothers and mothers-in-law can become commanding, even oppressive, figures while younger women are marginalized. There is a definite preference for male children, and girls are deprived of education and their life expectancy tends to be low. Interestingly, she noted, any progress towards bettering the life of women appears to be coming from the initiatives of men.

In Judaism, women are free and enjoy independence, both economically and socially. Today Jewish women tend to seek responsibility in the community. They are demanding a rereading of the texts that have been used to force them into secondary social and religious roles. Inequity in divorce is a concern because it is producing hardship for Jewish women in some nations.

In Chile, as the nation makes a transition to democracy, human rights issues are coming to the forefront, but there is no women's movement. Roman Catholicism is the majority religion, which means that women are to be subject to men and socially secondary. In 1989, the government instituted a Ministry of Women's Affairs, but women remain second-class citizens. Divorce is not allowed. "The old paradigm, 'Women work and men rule,' remains intact," said the Chilean representative.

In Peru, it was alleged, Christian evangelism lowered the status of women in society. Now, however, with the re-establishment of Peruvian culture, two things are happening: 1. Women are beginning to fill leadership positions; 2. Native religions are being restored.

SUMMARY. It can be said that women, regardless of religion or culture, continue to struggle and suffer in ways that men do not, simply because they are women. Illiteracy and lack of educational opportunities remain hindrances to progress. Religious fundamentalism is seen as restrictive and sexist. Many expressed the need for equity in divorce because of the hardship that comes to many women who experience this tragedy. Several women noted that women themselves must take personal responsibility for equality with men, regardless of their religious affiliation or current cultural climate.

We Christian women have a job to do. The answer is in the Message of Jesus Christ empowered by the Holy Spirit. The Church should be leading the way, elevating women to equality with me, even as Jesus did. (See my book, *10 Things Jesus Taught about Women.)*

6

Observations by The Host of the Colloquium

In closing the debate, M. Hervé Hasquin, who served as President of Wallonia-Brussels and as a university professor of history, presented eight points derived from his own research as well as from the remarks of women in the colloquium.

1. The history of women and religions is a history of the silencing of women. It is time to break that

silence. This is possible only in the context of political democracy.

2. In history, religion has always been a way of asserting one's identity when freedoms are denied. Women seek refuge in religion.

3. Women tend to be in denial regarding the restrictions placed on them by their religion.

4. Religion can be liberating for women, but restrictions normally arise based in tradition and fundamentalist expressions of that religion. Every case is unique, but economic and social contexts remains an influence on women's freedom.

5. When women experience advancement toward equality, men tend to feel deprived and to exhibit the need to return to those things that are certain. This gives rise to an increase in religious fundamentalism, which is perceived as a necessary defense against revolution.

6. In evaluating history, we must be moderate. The writing of history is a constant rewriting because the questions we ask in writing history are informed by our own context and we, therefore, search history on the basis of context-driven questions.

7. Ultimately, a person's relationship to faith is a personal issue.

8. The venue and nature of the symposium, with

> women from many different backgrounds, enabled each one to express themselves without imposing their believes and practice on the others.

M. Hasquin's final statement—his thesis, if you like—was that, in his informed opinion, in spite of its imperfections, the concept of separation of church and state remains fundamentally the best way to organize society.

I had carried with me a copy each of Eddie's book *(2000 Years of Charismatic Christianity)*, my book *(In the Spirit We're Equal)*, and my teaching manual (*The Spirit, The Bible, and Women—A Revival Perspective)*. As M. Hasquin was presenting his closing remarks, I felt that I should give him these copies. He graciously and enthusiastically accepted them.

7

My Contribution

Overview. Generally, throughout the day, the voice of the Christians seemed to me to be dull and inconsequential. One Protestant representative was almost shouted down at one point, but she rebounded with, "Just because I am a Protestant doesn't mean I should not be able to express my mind!"

Personally, I felt no such opposition. It seems, perhaps, that most of the people present did not know what a Pentecostal-Charismatic was and, therefore, at least out of curiosity, gave ear to what I had to say.

The assignment given me was to state briefly *where we are and where we are going as women in Pentecostal-Charismatic Christianity*. We know that a uniform trend is not obvious. Many Pentecostal-Charismatic women are embracing a traditional, subordinate role. But many, like myself, are unwilling to be disobedient to the Holy Spirit by obeying the dictates of distorted Christianity. We are discovering that Jesus taught the equality of men and women in every respect, including substance and value, privilege and responsibility, function and authority. We are uncovering the truth of biblical equality and we are proclaiming it far and wide by every possible means. Nevertheless, we are not driven by such a cause; rather, we are seeking to be led by the Spirit in all that we do. Following, then, is what I shared during the colloquium.

The Round Table Discussion

In the round table discussion, I was free to say whatever I wanted to say, and I had a clear sense of what that needed to be.

The moderator immediately opened the door for me to make a clear statement of the Gospel by asking me to define *Pentecostalism.* In the entire event, no one else was asked to clarify their religion. Again, at the conclusion of the round table, the moderator reminded me to reiterate the definition of *Pentecostalism* in the TV debate. In fact, his first question to me in the debate was, "What is *Pentecostalism?*"

Here, in essence, is what I said.

> *A Pentecostal-Charismatic* is a believer who has a born-again experience with Jesus Christ and an ongoing, dynamic experience of the presence and power of His Holy Spirit in life.
>
> In the history of Christianity, there have been two streams: Institutional Christianity and Pentecostal-Charismatic Christianity. I lay these out clearly in the "Women in Ministry" entry in the *Encyclopedia of Christian Civilization.* The institutional stream

has always tended to be hierarchical and to restrict women. The Pentecostal-Charismatic stream has always tended toward egalitarian relationships and equality for women.

Due to the 20th century global explosion of Pentecostal-Charismatic Christianity, there are now 600 million Pentecostal-Charismatics worldwide. In the United States, 20% of women profess to be Pentecostal-Charismatic Christians.

As a Pentecostal-Charismatic woman in America, I enjoy unfettered freedom to advance the truth of biblical equality according to Scripture. Those of us who profess a Pentecostal-Charismatic experience, know in our hearts by the indwelling Holy Spirit that we are equal with men in terms of substance and value, privilege and responsibility, function and authority. Because of cultural and religious baggage, however, most of us do not know this truth in our heads. This discrepancy between head and heart is the cause of many struggles for Pentecostal-Charismatic women. My job is to present the biblical truth that brings harmony between the head and heart.

To this end, my husband and I teach, write, and operate a publishing company. His first major book, *2000 Years of Charismatic Christianity*, [I held it up for all to see] validates the existence of the Pentecostal-Charismatic stream of Christianity as opposed to the institutional stream. My book, *In the Spirit We're Equal*, and my course, *The Spirit, The Bible, and Women* [I held them up for all to see] present the historical and biblical arguments for gender equality.

Others are also advancing this truth among Pentecostal-Charismatics. For example, the leading periodical for women in the movement in the United States is *Spirit Led Women* [I held up a copy for all to see]. You will notice a recent lead article entitled "10 Lies the Church Tells Women" by J. Lee Grady, a well-known Pentecostal-Charismatic author. This is an example of a partnership that is developing among some Pentecostal-Charismatic men and women to bring about biblical equality for women.

Also serving in various ways to advance the truth of equality throughout the Pentecostal-Charismatic Movement are two organizations: Christians for Biblical Equality and the Society for Pentecostal Studies.

Generally speaking, we are seeing two important advancements. Slowly, we are seeing a release from gender-defined roles for women to gift-defined living. And we are seeing a greater sense of equal partnership between men and women.

We are seeing an increase in Pentecostal-Charismatic women taking leadership positions in various areas such as communication and the arts, education (including theological education), business and technology, law and government. Pentecostal-Charismatic women are also gaining influence in dealing with domestic abuse, pastoral counseling, and medical concerns.

The one great stronghold of inequality among Pentecostal-Charismatic believers is the home. I, for one, am working to bring the equality Jesus taught to this important area.

The TV Debate

During the TV debate, the moderator asked me three questions.

QUESTION 1. What is a *Pentecostal-Charismatic?*

MY ANSWER. *A Pentecostal-Charismatic* is a believer who has a born-again experience with Jesus Christ and an ongoing, dynamic experience of the presence and power of His Holy Spirit in life.

In the history of Christianity, there have been two streams: Institutional Christianity and Pentecostal-Charismatic Christianity. The institutional stream has always tended to be hierarchical and to restrict women.

The Pentecostal-Charismatic stream has always tended toward egalitarian relationships and gender equality.

Due to the 20th century global explosion of Pentecostal-Charismatic Christianity, there are now 600 million P/Cs worldwide. In the United States, 20% of women profess to be Pentecostal-Charismatic Christians.

QUESTION 2. What is the greatest area of struggle for Pentecostal-Charismatic women?

MY ANSWER. The greatest struggle for Pentecostal-Charismatic women is the process of renewing their minds in the knowledge that they are equal with men. Changing the mind is one of the greatest struggles we all encounter, and I would say that this is the crux of the struggle for both men and women in Pentecostal-Charismatic Christianity, whether they realize it or not. What we think about women determines our behavior in relation to womanhood.

QUESTION 3. George W. Bush, a professing Christian, has recently been elected President of the United States. What is the position of Pentecostal-Charismatic women in relation to liberal and conservative, Democratic and Republican politics?

MY ANSWER. That is a question I do not feel I can answer adequately. I am a citizen of Heaven and a citizen of Canada, but I am privileged to reside legally in the United States. I know several Pentecostal-

Charismatic women who are active at various levels in the political arena, but I am not adequately versed in that subject to be able to answer your question.

The Power of His Presence In Us Who Believe

I phoned Eddie to update him on the day's events. I told him that I felt I had been there to give a clear, concise statement of the Gospel and that this statement had been called forth three times by the moderator of the round table and the TV debate. It was the ONLY time that the Gospel was proclaimed in the entire event.

I did express my concern to Eddie that I had not been able to say enough. When I said that, immediately I had a message in tongues. On the other end of the line in Texas, Eddie had the interpretation. Essentially, the word of the Lord was that if I had, in fact, said nothing, the sheer fact of my presence was enough because He was present through my presence. Just as the Presence of God caused the pagan god, Dagan, to fall, (1 Samuel 5:1-5), there are times when our presence as believers is enough.

My! How the Holy Spirit met me! It was liberating. It was peaceable. My anxiety evaporated in His Presence! Praise the Lord!

8

Reflections

A few observations. I have been listening to the Lord about why He had me there and what He would have me to learn, say, or do as a result. Here are a few thoughts.

1. Christian women need to shake off the shackles of religion masquerading as biblical Christianity. Much of what is taught about womanhood among Pentecostal-Charismatic Christians is no different from what is taught in various other religions. For example, the idea of male authoritative rulership and female subordination, servanthood, and subjugation is a characteristic of religion. It is not a legitimate principle of biblical, Spirit-filled Christianity.

2. The favor of man over woman is typical of religion, but not of Jesus.

3. Spirit-filled women must take personal responsibility to develop their abilities, gifts, and talents, including their intellectual ability through educational opportunities. This is a responsibility, not a privilege, and must not be left to men alone.

4. Women in all religions are struggling because of

doctrines that teach the primacy of the male. Marriage is, perhaps, the main stronghold of inequity. Divorce that favors men seems to be a global problem. (Addendum: Over the past decade, I have noticed that the scales have tipped the other way in some countries. Decisions of this sort should not be determined by gender, but other important factors.)

5. Women in all religions have gender-defined roles that provide them with social power of some sort. This social structure inevitably produces a climate of manipulation by women which produces power for a few and hopeless depression for many others.

There is no reason why, in this era of Pentecostal-Charismatic outpouring of God's Holy Spirit, that we should succumb to religion. We must realize that the Spirit of God does not come to confirm that what we believe about everything is right and that what other Christians believe is wrong. Rather, the Spirit comes to help us in our human weakness, to empower us, to comfort us. And the Spirit comes to guide us into all truth! That is to say, the Spirit comes to open our understanding and to help us change the way we think.

It is my prayer that we will allow the Spirit of God to change the way we, who profess to be Spirit-Filled Christians, think about womanhood. May we shed our religious thinking and think about womanhood the way Jesus wants us to think! And, according to the Gospels and all of Scripture accurately interpreted, that means thinking of women as equal with men in terms of substance and value, privilege and responsibility, function and authority in all areas of life and leadership, ministry and marriage. He has gifted each of us for His purpose.

AN OVERLOOKED MISSION FIELD. In my brief encounter with the French Community of Wallonia-Brussels in the new European Union, I sensed the dynamic power that always seems to accompany a new venture. The EU is in its formative years. It is looking ahead to what it can become. It is searching for the best way to order its society. This is refreshing! But are Spirit-filled Christians as aware and alert to the need and to the opportunity as are those of other persuasions? Europe has had enough of the Christian religion. Now they must see Jesus!

I have often said that many Christians will go to the ends of the earth to reach the uneducated masses. This is good! But will they go next door to reach the educated feminist who is turned off by patriarchal Christian religion? I have no doubt that the EU's French community in Belgium is genuinely concerned about women—including the feminist—and about what role religion should play in advancing the equality of women in their state and the emerging European Union. What a place for the Presence of God through people who can rub shoulders with the decision-makers!

Regardless of the teaching of some Christian prophecy teachers regarding the EU, perhaps the Church should embrace the fact that something that will influence the future is, in fact, emerging in Europe. And instead of smugly dismissing the EU as an emerging evil empire, perhaps we should dismiss our own stagnation and take a lesson from our European friends.

Perhaps we should examine North American Pentecostal-Charismatic Christianity and realize that our methods need to be brought back to the standard and means of Jesus Christ. The fruit of our authority structures and spiritual formation methods reek of religion and have little scent of Heaven!

Perhaps we should be less concerned about music and entertainment, and about flamboyant preachers with extra-biblical theologies. Perhaps we should be less concerned about funding TV programs and building cathedrals and networks of personal power.

I have no doubt that the Lord wants us to purge the message we teach and preach so that it comes into line with the Message of Jesus. I have no doubt that the only means the Lord would have us use is the power of the Holy Spirit. Everything else is secondary, superfluous, and a hindrance.

I hope this report has troubled you, challenged you, and inspired you! And perhaps Mary's words in John 2:5 can take on new significance for each of us: **"Whatever He [Jesus] says to you, do it!"**

9

An Unexpected Adventure Of Another Kind!

Following the events of the day, I slept for 3 hours and was then chauffeured to the airport to catch my early flight to Dallas-Fort Worth International Airport via Newark.

At the Continental Airlines ticket counter, I showed my ticket and passport. But my excitement turned to horror when the ticket agent asked to see my U. S. Resident Alien Card! Suddenly it hit me! I had not put it in the purse I was using on this, my weekend excursion to Europe!

The ticket agent explained that, if they allowed me to board the flight, the airline would be fined $10,000. But she proceeded to investigate possible options. First, she rebooked me for the same flight the next morning. Then she advised me to take the train or a taxi to the American Embassy in downtown Brussels to get a travel letter. At this point, I had 24 hours and $100 to resolve my dilemma!

And I was now forced to learn some things about Belgium. How does this peculiar money work? How much do things cost? Do I want water *with gas* or the kind *without gas?* Where do I get the train? How do I get a taxi? How much will it cost? Who can I ask? It was a learning opportunity that would have been much easier if I had had adequate rest the previous night!

Well, I discovered that I had enough money to get to the U. S. Embassy, so I boarded the train for 9 francs and disembarked at the 3rd station (Central Station) in downtown Brussels. From there I found the taxi stand and handed over whatever that cost!

But, to my amazement, the Embassy was not able to help me. First, they said they could do nothing because I had not lost my alien registration card. Then they decided they could process me again, issuing a new card. But that would cost $200 (which I did not have!), 3 photos, and at least 2 days! Since I had no money for hotels, and was, by this time, very much in need of rest, this would not work!

I left the Embassy with my tail between my legs and a sob choking my throat. What could I do?

A kind American security guard, recognizing my quiet distress, ordered me a taxi and helped me count my money to see if I had enough left to get back to the airport. I did!

Once back to square one, I learned to use my AT & T

prepaid phone card and phoned Eddie in Texas to see if he could locate my alien registration card. Yes! He found it!

He then went to the Continental desk at DFW and they faxed it along with a note clarifying the situation. In the meantime, Eddie banked the money he had received from weekend ministry in Tulsa, OK, and Powderly, TX, so that I would have access to some money on our Visa Bank Card.

A hotel room, at $300 a night, was still out of the question, so I walked the Brussels airport for 24 hours. Had I not already been suffering from sleep deprivation, this wouldn't have been so tough! But, by 10 PM, I was VERY tired and KNEW I needed prayer reinforcement. (Thank you for your prayers! I know they helped me through the night!)

Don't you know that I was first in line when Continental opened at 6:30 on Tuesday morning!

Yes, the faxed copy had come through, but they would not know if it were acceptable until it could be approved by someone in authority on the incoming flight. More waiting and trusting! Finally, the answer came. NO! The faxed copy was not acceptable! (We have learned since that it should have been.)

The Continental ticket agents continued to look for options. I suggested that if they could get me a direct flight to DFW, Eddie could meet me at the gate with my alien registration card. Pursuing this option, they found a flight with Sabena, the Belgium Airline, and it would leave at 10:15 AM. HALLELUJAH!

Now my only challenge was the cost of the new ticket. (Remember! The Belgium government had covered my expenses, which had meant that I could, in fact, accept their invitation.) The Sabena flight cost $553 in US funds. (This was money we were planning to use to pay bills, so it was a difficult decision! But I really had no choice!) So, I could handle the price of a new ticket now, whereas on Monday morning (Brussels time), there had been no money available in our accounts!

I arrived at DFW that same afternoon at 2:30. Can you imagine my relief? Can you imagine my delight when, as I was leaving the plane, the flight attendant handed me that precious *green card?*

(P.S. Ladies, be sure that when you switch purses, you move ALL of the important contents from the one to the other!)

About the Author

Dr. Susan Stubbs Hyatt (b. 1946) is a Bible scholar, church historian, ordained minister (1983), author, administrator, and life-long, professional educator.

After graduating from the University of New Brunswick Teachers College in 1966, she spent several years teaching public school and college in New Brunswick, Canada. She then served as a Certified Life Coach in the local college, followed by graduation from Christ for the Nations Institute in Dallas, Texas, in 1976, and *summa cum laude* from Southwestern Assemblies of God University in 1987. She then earned two M.A.s *with honors* from the Oral Roberts University Graduate School of Theology and Missions, one in Historical and Theological Studies (1989); the other, in Biblical Studies (1994). She did a year of post-graduate studies at the Center for Advanced Theological Studies at Fuller Theological Seminary (1994-95) in Pasadena, California, and received her Doctor of Ministry degree from the School of Divinity at Regent

University in 2000. Dr. Hyatt is the recipient of many academic awards, such as WHO'S WHO Among Students, The National Religion and Philosophy Award, National Dean's Honors List, Academic All American, and *Delta Epsilon Chi* (Honor Society of the American Association of Bible Colleges).

She is a published author. In addition to her own books, she contributed the chapter "Spirit-Filled Women" in the benchmark publication, *The Century of the Holy Spirit*. She contributed the "Women in Ministry" entry to the *Encyclopedia of Christian Civilization*, published by Blackwell (Oxford and Boston) in 2008, and she and Eddie were contributors to the *Revival Bible* edited by Winkey Pratney.

In 2001, she was the sole representative of Pentecostal-Charismatic women of North America at the *Women in Religion Colloquium* in Brussels. She has also ministered throughout her native land of Canada, in various European nations, including Bulgaria, England, Sweden, Ireland, as well as in Nigeria and Ghana in Africa, and in Meghalaya, India and Jakarta, Indonesia.

As an advocate of Biblical manhood and womanhood and Biblical equality, she is the founding director of the International Christian Women's Hall of Fame and serves as president of God's Word to Women, Inc.

Sue and her husband, Dr. Eddie L. Hyatt, are equal partners in ministry and marriage.

Mailing Address: P. O. Box 3877, Grapevine, TX 76099
Email Address: DrSueHyatt@live.com

Other Resources

Some of the Books Published
by
The Int'l Christian Women's Hall of Fame
September 2019

SERIES 1: WOMEN OF THE GALLERY

- Dr. Katherine Bushnell by Susan Stubbs Hyatt
- Lilian Thistlethwaite by Linda Miller
- Where Are My Susannas? By Susan Stubbs Hyatt
- Compendium: Women of The Gallery (coming soon)

SERIES 2: THIS IS MY STORY

- Discovering Truth: My Journey As a Woman in the Church by Susan Stubbs Hyatt
- Others are in process! Coming Soon!

SERIES 3: STUDIES IN SCRIPTURE

- Paul, Women, and Church by Eddie L. Hyatt
- Who's The Boss: A Liberating Look at Ephesians 5:21-33 by Eddie L. Hyatt
- In the Spirit We're Equal: The Spirit, The Bible, and Women—A Revival Perspective by Susan Stubbs Hyatt (Reprint coming in late 2019)
- God's Word to Women by Katherine Bushnell Available at The Hall and www.godswordtowomen.org

These are available in Kindle and Paperback
at amazon.com and at The Hall of Fame Bookstore.

The Int'l Christian Women's Hall of Fame

Celebrating God's Women of Yesterday and Creating World Changers for a Better Tomorrow

The Hall offers an Exhibit Hall, Research Library, Bookstore, TV Studio, Seminars and Courses, Induction Presentations, GWTW Publishing, and a Sunday Fellowship, both onsite and online. Guided tours are available upon request.

The Hall is sponsored solely by the donations of the "time, talent, and treasure" of Friends and Partners of God's Word to Women, Inc. (1998) and Hyatt Int'l Ministries, Inc. (1984), both of which are 501(c)3, non-profit organizations, duly registered with the IRS. The Hall invites your financial partnership, as well as donations of pictures, books, videos and audio recordings, and other items to grow The Hall.

Founding Director of The Hall is Dr. Susan Stubbs Hyatt who oversees daily operations and enjoys the help of the Executive Board and the Board of Advisers.

The Hall is an educational center serving as the premier center for Conservative Christian Women's Studies.

LOCATION: 909 S. Main St, Ste. 107, Grapevine, TX 76051

MAILING ADDRESS: P. O. Box 3877, Grapevine, TX 76099

EMAIL: DrSueHyatt@live.com

WEB SITES

www.godswordtowomen.org

www.gwtwChristianWomensHallofFame.com

FACEBOOK:

https://www.facebook.com/groups/godswordtowomen/

https://www.facebook.com/groups/IntChristianWomensHallofFame

Made in the USA
Columbia, SC
07 December 2021